Garfield
Flying High

JIM DAVIS

ℛℛ
RAVETTE BOOKS

This edition first published by
Ravette Books Limited 1988
Reprinted 1988, 1989

Printed and bound in Great Britain
for Ravette Books Limited,
3 Glenside Estate, Star Road, Partridge Green,
Horsham, West Sussex RH13 8RA
by Cox & Wyman Ltd, Reading

ISBN 1 85304 043 6

© 1987 United Feature Syndicate, Inc.

© 1987 United Feature Syndicate, Inc.

© 1987 United Feature Syndicate, Inc.

© 1987 United Feature Syndicate, Inc.

© 1987 United Feature Syndicate, Inc.

© 1987 United Feature Syndicate, Inc.

© 1987 United Feature Syndicate, Inc.

© 1987 United Feature Syndicate, Inc.

WHAT DOES ONE
HAVE TO DO TO GET
ONE'S BELLY SCRATCHED
AROUND HERE?

JIM DAVIS   8-11

© 1987 United Feature Syndicate, Inc.

JIM DAVIS 8-14

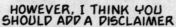

© 1987 United Feature Syndicate, Inc.

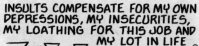

© 1987 United Feature Syndicate, Inc.

JIM DAVIS

10-5

© 1987 United Feature Syndicate, Inc.

JIM DAVIS

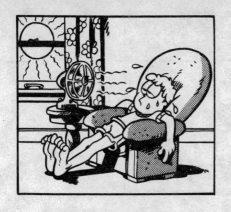

9-14

JIM DAVIS

© 1987 United Feature Syndicate, Inc.

© 1987 United Feature Syndicate, Inc.

ARE YOU EVER SERIOUS, GARFIELD?

I GUESS NOT

IT'S HARD TO BE SERIOUS WHEN YOU'RE NAKED!

OTHER GARFIELD BOOKS IN THIS SERIES

No. 1	Garfield The Great Lover	£1.95
No. 2	Garfield Why Do You Hate Mondays?	£1.95
No. 3	Garfield Does Pooky Need You?	£1.95
No. 4	Garfield Admit It, Odie's OK!	£1.95
No. 5	Garfield Two's Company	£1.95
No. 6	Garfield What's Cooking?	£1.95
No. 7	Garfield Who's Talking?	£1.95
No. 8	Garfield Strikes Again	£1.95
No. 9	Garfield Here's Looking At You	£1.95
No. 10	Garfield We Love You Too	£1.95
No. 11	Garfield Here We Go Again	£1.95
No. 12	Garfield Life and Lasagne	£1.95
No. 13	Garfield In The Pink	£1.95
No. 14	Garfield Just Good Friends	£1.95
No. 15	Garfield Plays It Again	£1.95
No. 17	Garfield On Top Of The World	£1.95
No. 18	Garfield Happy Landings	£1.95

LANDSCAPE SERIES

Garfield The All-Round Sports Star	£2.95
Garfield The Irresistible	£2.95
Garfield On Vacation	£2.95
Garfield Weighs In!	£2.95
Garfield I Hate Monday	£2.95
Garfield Special Delivery	£2.95
Garfield The Incurable Romantic	£2.95
Garfield Another Serve	£2.95
Garfield Wraps It Up	£2.95
Garfield This Is Your Life	£2.95
Garfield Sheer Genius	£2.95
Garfield Goes Wild	£2.95

COLOUR TV SPECIALS

Here Comes Garfield	£2.95
Garfield On The Town	£2.95
Garfield In The Rough	£2.95
Garfield In Disguise	£2.95
Garfield In Paradise	£2.95
Garfield Goes To Hollywood	£2.95
A Garfield Christmas	£2.95

COLOUR TREASURIES

The Second Garfield Treasury	£5.95
The Third Garfield Treasury	£5.95
The Fourth Garfield Treasury	£5.95

Garfield A Weekend Away	£4.95
Garfield Book Of Cat Names	£2.50
Garfield Best Ever	£4.95
Garfield Selection	£5.95
Garfield How To Party	£3.95
Garfield, The Easter Bunny?	£3.95

All these books are available at your local bookshop or newsagent, or can be ordered direct from the publisher. Just tick the titles you require and fill in the form below. Prices and availability subject to change without notice.

Ravette Books Limited, 3 Glenside Estate, Star Road, Partridge Green, Horsham, West Sussex RH13 8RA

Please send a cheque or postal order and allow the following for postage and packing. UK: Pocket-books – 45p for up to two books and 15p for each additional book. Landscape Series, TV Specials and Cat Names – 45p for one book plus 15p for each additional book. Other titles – 75p for each book.

Name ....

Address ....

....